BUILDING YOUR
STRENGTHS

women of faith™

BUILDING YOUR STRENGTHS

BY

KATE ETUE

FOREWORD BY

PATSY CLAIRMONT

THOMAS NELSON
Since 1798

© 2009 by Thomas Nelson

Previously Published as *Embracing Your Strengths*

The publishers are grateful to Kate Etue for her collaboration, writing skills, and editorial help in developing the content for this book.

Published in Nashville, Tennessee, by Thomas Nelson. Thomas Nelson is a trademark of HarperCollins Christian Publishing, Inc.

Thomas Nelson title may be purchased in bulk for educational, business, fundraising, or sales promotional use. For information, please e-mail SpecialMarkets@ ThomasNelson.com.

ISBN: 978-0-3106-8269-1

First Printing August 2016 / Printed in the United States of America

✒ Contents ✒

✒ FOREWORD ✒

"If God sends us on strong paths,
we are provided strong shoes."

—Corrie Ten Boom

Girls, let me just say it right up front—yes, you do have gifts! And yes, you are stronger than you think!

Whew! That feels better.

For some reason we gals have trouble embracing these truths. Many (most) of us underestimate our value and our strength and we buy into the cheap lie that we were on holiday when the gifts and grit were handed out. Hardly.

Take me for instance . . . every year I have to turn to my friends to be reminded that I am a competent speaker. No kidding. I have been speaking for over thirty years and I still get the knee-knocking jitters. You'd think by my age I'd be more confident. But these are the thoughts that bounce through my brain: What if my message isn't well received? What if I forget what I was going to say? What if I'm just too old and blather on? These doubts become battering rams against my best intentions.

The thing that helps me survive my own insecurities is understanding my God-given gifts and strengths, rehearsing God's faithfulness, and receiving my friends' affirmation. As an ex-agoraphobic, I know what it's like to feel three ribbons short of a gift. I was certain I had been overlooked. I didn't realize my gab was a gift. Because it's a funny thing about gifts—we usually don't consider ours as unique or as stunning as someone else's gift, because whatever ours is, it comes so easily to us that we don't get the big deal about it.

My timid friend Carol is a wonderful artist, but for years we couldn't convince her of it. Art naturally flowed through everything she did (decorating her house, cooking a meal, loving her family, painting life on a canvas), so she didn't get the gift part for a long time. Then one day she signed up for an art class at a large art supply store and after the first class they hired her to train their instructors. Not their students mind you, but their instructors. She was dumbfounded. We, her friends, gloated. And you know what happened when she began owning and living her gift? Not only did she grow as an artist, but she grew stronger internally.

Somehow gifts and strength work that way. It's as if one blesses the other. There's just something about finding out where we fit into the rhythms of the universe that is deeply satisfying and that infuses us with confidence in the way God has created us. Gifts and strength add to our life purpose.

Just as surely as God pressed the stars in the heavens to be His light-holders, He has positioned us with gifts to shine for Him. So don't be shy—step up and acknowledge the generosity of God toward you by functioning in your strengths. And don't let your fragile self-esteem (we all own one) keep you from the healing joy of your divinely-inspired place—as God's gift holder. Shine, my friend, shine!

Remember: Yes, you do have gifts! And yes, you are stronger than you think!

From one who knows,
—*Patsy Clairmont*

⚡ INTRODUCTION ⚡

There's something profoundly beautiful in the timeworn face, cotton-soft hands, and deep, searching eyes of an elderly woman. Each wrinkle stands as a monument to one of life's joys or tragedies. Each age spot is testimony to another year of experience and grace. When you look into the richness of her eyes, you see the events of years, both devastating and delightful, that have shaped the woman she is. In her you see wisdom, patience, and strength.

But strength is not reserved for the elderly, is it? Margaret Thatcher, as one of the United Kingdom's most prolific Prime Ministers, had to maintain a firm stance to ensure the safety and status of her country in the world during the Cold War. Angelina Jolie is not only the essence of physical strength, with toned arms and a daring spirit, but she has shown that it is possible to balance both motherhood and a successful career while also crusading to make a difference in the world. And you probably know countless others who have looked tragedy in the eye and refused to succumb to the alluring darkness of self-pity and despair, but instead have risen up and celebrated life and hope in one way or another.

As Frederich Nietzsche said, "What does not destroy me, makes me stronger." Becoming a woman of deep strength is not an easy thing. It can be a journey fraught with difficulty and frustration, if not deep sadness and heartache. But the satisfaction and contentment that comes from knowing that you have access to the unending wells of divine strength are truly a gift from God.

So step back, take a deep breath, and look closely at your life. What has made you stronger? How have those things given you strength? If you can identify these movements in your spirit and see the ways that they make you strong, you can more effectively use your strengths to be a woman whose life ultimately glorifies Jesus Christ.

My flesh and my heart fail; But God is the strength of my heart and my portion forever.

—Psalm 73:26

He gives strength to the weary
and increases the power
of the weak.

Isaiah 40:29 NIV

CHAPTER ONE

INTELLECTUAL STRENGTH

JESUS SAID TO HIM, "YOU SHALL LOVE THE LORD YOUR GOD WITH ALL YOUR HEART, WITH ALL YOUR SOUL, AND WITH ALL YOUR MIND."

Matthew 22:37

We have each been given a precious gift, more valuable than jewelry from Tiffany & Co. or a luxury vacation to the French Riviera. That gift is our minds. Our ability to reason sets us apart from the rest of creation. Because of our intellect we are able to choose favorite songs, create art, organize messy closets, calculate which box of diapers gives us the best value, and carry on a conversation with a friend. And, because we are women of faith, we are also called to evaluate all those things in light of our beliefs—another aspect of our intellect.

"A mind is a terrible thing to waste" has been the slogan for the United Negro College Fund for more than three decades, and its truth is so pervasive that it has become a common American saying. We should care for our minds the same way we should maintain our homes, nurture our children, and exercise our bodies. We wouldn't let piles of junk line the halls of our homes, so why

CLEARING ⚹ THE ⚹ COBWEBS

We wouldn't let piles of junk line the halls of our homes, so why should we allow negative thoughts and old resentments to gather in the recesses of our minds?

should we allow negative thoughts and old resentments to gather in the recesses of our minds? We wouldn't ignore our children, letting them fend for themselves in a fallen world without care and guidance, so why do we think we can make it through life without the guidance of those with more experience? We know we should exercise our bodies and eat healthy foods, so we should do the same for our minds—challenging ourselves mentally through brain exercises like crossword puzzles as well as sharpening our intellect through deep, thoughtful conversation.

1. Describe your idea of an intelligent woman. Consider 1 Samuel 25:3, 2 Chronicles 2:12, Daniel 5:14, and Acts 13:7 in your response.

2. While the Bible promises that we are intelligent people, created in God's own image, it also tells us that we are limited in our ability to understand God and the world. Describe the way God limits and expands our understanding of Himself in light of Isaiah 44:18 and Luke 24:45.

3. As Christians, we must understand the law God gives us in his Word. It is a gift to us, and if we fail to learn it we won't be able to follow it. Some of us are able to memorize huge portions of Scripture; others read it so often that it becomes instinct. Fill in the blanks in these two verses, then explain the significance of the difference between the two passages.

"Therefore you shall lay up these _____ of mine in your _____ and in your _____, and bind them as a sign on your hand, and they shall be as frontlets between your _____" (Deuteronomy 11:18).

"For this is the covenant that _____ will make . . . says the Lord: _____ will put My laws in their _____ and write them on their _____; and I will be their _____, and they shall be My people" (Hebrews 8:10).

Our intellect allows us to function in this world—to do business, decorate a home, raise children, maintain relationships, and more. But it is also, in many ways, the seat of our spiritual life. We must know God to love God. Without an understanding of who He is, there can be no relationship.

Likewise, our thoughts in many ways influence and determine our actions. Millions of people have attempted to understand the power their minds have over their circumstances. But the connection is ages old. In Matthew 12:34–35 Jesus said, "Out of the overflow of the heart the mouth speaks. The good man brings good things out of the good stored up in him, and the evil man brings evil things out of the evil stored up in him" (NIV). If we let our intellect fade and numb our minds with useless things, that is what will come out of us in the form of words, ideas, or actions.

4. Read Romans 12:2. Why is it important for us to have a sharp mind and intellect?

5. According to Romans 1:28, what will happen to us if we ignore the knowledge God allows us to share in?

6. God tells us that He will search our minds and know our deepest thoughts. How does this make you feel? Match up the verses with the promises below.

BIBLE PASSAGE	PROMISE
1 Chronicles 28:9	God searches our minds to reward us.
Jeremiah 17:10	If you seek God, you will find Him.
Romans 8:6	God is in control of our wisdom and intelligence.
1 Corinthians 1:19	The mind controlled by the spirit is life and peace.

Although God has graciously given us the ability to think for ourselves, that gift comes with a price. We have free will to make our own choices in this life—to choose God or reject Him. We cannot be ignorant of the consequences of our choices. And it's crucial that we understand the precarious position we hold in this world.

7. Paul tells us that our minds are weak — that they are able to be deceived and need to be protected. According to these verses, what must we do to protect our minds?

Romans 16:18–20

1 Corinthians 14:15

Isaiah 26:3

2 Corinthians 10:5

8. Read Philippians 4:7. What is the benefit of exercising our minds in the things of God?

We know we should exercise our bodies and eat healthy foods, so we should do the same for our minds. If we let our intellect fade and numb our minds with useless things, that is what will come out of us in the form of words, ideas, or actions.

DIGGING DEEPER

If intellect is one of your strengths, you're probably hyper-aware of the failings of yourself and others. Protect yourself from being overly critical by thinking daily on the promises that we are all God's creation and live for His glory, not our own. Read Isaiah 43:7 each morning this week.

PONDER & PRAY

Focus your prayers this week on the things you know to be true about God. In what ways is He the greatest Intellect? As you are made in His image, how does that intelligence flow down to you? And what will you do about it? Ask God to show you His will for your life when it comes to your mind. How are you to use your thoughts to glorify God—in big ways or small? How will you use your intellect to make a difference in this world?

TRINKETS TO TREASURE

At the close of each lesson, you will be presented with a small gift. Though imaginary, it will serve to remind you of the things you have learned. Think of it as a souvenir! Souvenirs are little trinkets we pick up on our journeys to remind us of where we have been. They keep us from forgetting the path we have travelled. Hide these little treasures in your heart, for as you ponder on them, they will draw you closer to God!

This week's trinket is a graduation cap and tassel, to help remind us to exercise and care for our minds. One way we can do this is by picking a Bible verse to memorize this week. This may be the theme verse for this chapter, Matthew 22:37, or it could be a favorite verse you turn to often. Memorization boosts your mental strength, so practice it often!

Notes & Prayer Requests

_____

_____

_____

_____

_____

_____

_____

_____

_____

_____

_____

_____

_____

_____

_____

_____

_____

_____

_____

_____

_____

_____

CHAPTER TWO

RELATIONAL STRENGTH

AS IRON SHARPENS IRON, SO A MAN SHARPENS THE COUNTENANCE OF HIS FRIEND.

Proverbs 27:17

here is nothing so comforting as a friend who knows how to love you. She knows when you need words of encouragement and when you just need a quiet place to speak your troubles freely. She knows how to make you laugh and what makes you cry. A good friend is one of the best parts of life.

When things are going well in our relationships, we're generally doing well also. And when there are problems in those relationships, it's usually quite obvious. Our friends can hurt us as well as heal, and it's important to understand the inner workings of our relationships so we can avoid creating painful emotions for those we love. God has given us each other to walk with in our spiritual journeys. But relationships are hard, and many marriages and friendships break down over time. If we hold onto the baggage of our life instead of trusting in the forgiveness and grace of God in our relationships, we have no chance of growing as a friend.

CLEARING ↗ THE ↖ COBWEBS

God has given us each other to walk with in our spiritual journeys. But our friends can hurt us as well as heal, and it's important to understand our relationships to avoid creating painful emotions for those we love.

A good friend is one who trusts, understands, gives space, and is willing to speak honestly into your life. And if we can get to the place where we can truly serve others in love, as the Bible commands, we'll escape the traps of jealousy, betrayal, and anger that plague so many relationships.

1. What makes a person a good friend? Proverbs 17:9, 17; 18:24; 27:6, 9; and 27:10 each give us great insight into friendship. List some thoughts in the space below.

2. As we move through the various stages of our lives — childhood, teenage years, single life, newlywed years, parenthood, and empty nesting — we meet and develop friendships with people whom we relate to at those particular times. What advice do the following Scripture verses give about making new friends?

Proverbs 12:26

Micah 7:5

1 Corinthians 15:33

3. True friends are loyal to each other in good times and bad. That can be the most challenging aspect of a relationship — expressing happiness for your joyous friend when you're suffering heartache, or finding compassion and tact for a hurting friend when you're bubbling over with excitement in your own life. How does Mark 5:19 instruct those in each of these situations?

4. Words are like weapons — they can wound a friend deeply and permanently. We must remember that we walk around armed with dangerous tools that can hurt and destroy. Likewise, God's Word is like a double-edged sword, penetrating deep in a healing way (Hebrews 4:12). Speaking the truth of God into a friend's life can be a uniting act or a divisive one, depending on the way you approach it. Read the following verses and jot down what they have to say about the power of words in relationships.

Proverbs 16:28

Proverbs 27:6, 9

Ephesians 4:15

Hebrews 10:24

3 John 14

Our lives have become incredibly fast paced. We're racing from work to practice to dinner with friends and back home to finish up chores and check the latest posts on social media while watching TV before hitting the bed much later than we had planned. We're exhausted, and we're too tired to do anything about it. But think back to those days long ago—before cell phones, online social networks, e-mail, and a dozen blogs to check daily. When you spoke to people face to face rather than online, did you feel a deeper connection?

It's easy to feel isolated in the "communication age" because we've become so accustomed to communicating with people that we have little relationship with. As we spread ourselves thin relationally, even our deepest friendships can feel the strain.

5. Read Exodus 33:11, Proverbs 17:17, and Galatians 5:13. How do you build relationships in a fast-paced world? What specific actions can you take to deepen the intimacy level of a few friendships to intentionally make them more significant?

6. The Bible is full of stories of faithless friends, yet they are still identified as "friends" not "enemies." Match the Scripture passage below with the act of betrayal.

BIBLE PASSAGE	ACT OF BETRAYAL
Deuteronomy 13:6	Betrayed for selfish gain
2 Samuel 13:3	Failed to aid her when under attack
Esther 5:10	Abandoned out of fear
Lamentations 1:1–9	Suggested murder
Judges 16:1–20	Encouraged lust
Matthew 26:56, 58	Enticed into false worship

Why do you think God refers to these people as friends? What does this imply for us according to 2 Timothy 2:13?

7. Read 1 John 3:1a and John 15:14. What must we do to be friends of God? And how does that influence our human friendships?

Digging Deeper

Becoming a good friend takes practice, honesty, and time. This week, get together with a friend just to visit—listen to her heart, speak into her life, or just laugh together over life's hilarious events. Get real with a friend this week. Ask someone you know and trust to identify one area of your relationship that you could improve—do you regularly call at a really inconvenient time of day, or do you have a terrible habit of asking a question and then not waiting for an answer? Prepare yourself to hear this without feeling defensive, knowing that the counsel of a good friend is healing. And then relax and be patient, knowing that building a relationship is not an overnight process but a lifetime of give and take.

Ponder & Pray

Ask God to show you who in your life needs extra love and care this week. It may be your mom, your husband, a dear friend, or a child. Or it may be you. If you need the support of those in your life, don't be afraid to ask for it. And if you know of someone who could benefit from your time and attention, don't be too shy or selfish to give it.

Trinkets to Treasure

Our trinket this week is a friendship bracelet, to remind us of the bonds we've formed with others and the importance of relationships in our lives. This week, think of what is the most convenient way for you to connect with your friends—whether online, by phone, at the coffee-shop, or in the pick-up line at school. Find a new way to connect with a friend and see if you enjoy your new mode of communication. Also think of what you can do this week to strengthen other relationships in your life.

CHAPTER THREE

PROFESSIONAL STRENGTH

WHATEVER YOU DO, DO IT ALL FOR THE GLORY OF GOD.

1 Corinthians 10:31 NIV

Most great success stories contain some similarities to a rollercoaster ride. Consider the résumé of Joseph. His chronological job descriptions would read something like this: Favored son. Slave. First assistant to a high-ranking government official. Convicted felon. Chief Operating Officer of Egypt. Quite an up-and-down professional life, don't you think? Joseph was hired, fired, forgotten, and then went on to become the most powerful man in the nation of Egypt, second only to the pharaoh.

In our professional lives, we will always face challenges and setbacks, but if we choose to focus on them, we will miss out on the grand opportunities that also come our way. Joseph's life was full of God-ordained ups and downs, but through it all he was able to maintain integrity, perseverance, and kindness in all these situations.

CLEARING ↗ THE ↖ COBWEBS

In our professional lives, we will always face challenges and setbacks, but if we choose to focus on them, we will miss out on the grand opportunities that also come our way.

1. Think of someone whose professional life you have a high regard for. What about him or her do you most admire? How does he or she inspire you?

After Joseph's jealous brothers sold him into slavery, he ended up in the house of Potiphar, the captain of Pharaoh's guards. Before long, Joseph's work was so excellent that Potiphar entrusted Joseph with control of his whole household. What an amazing compliment to the integrity of his work! Of course, not everyone appreciated his integrity—Potiphar's wife took notice of young, handsome Joseph and decided that she liked what she saw. She pursued him and wouldn't take no for an answer. Joseph's continued refusal of her advances made her angry, so she claimed Joseph attacked her and had him sent to prison.

2. Read Genesis 39:4–6. Would your employer say that he or she is blessed to have you as an employee? What traits might Joseph have displayed in order to receive such a glowing report?

3. When propositioned by Potiphar's wife, Joseph didn't say, "No way! Can you imagine what would happen if Potiphar found out?" Instead, he said, "'How could I do such a wicked thing and sin against God?'" (Genesis 39:9 NIV). Joseph knew that he was ultimately in the service of the Lord, not Potiphar. How can Joseph's perspective—that we are ultimately working for the Lord—influence our perspective of work?

4. How might this perspective of working for God, and not man, influence the integrity of your work?

Lingering in prison, serving time for a false accusation, Joseph had plenty of opportunity to become bitter and cynical. But instead, we see that Joseph's integrity was once again recognized and he was put in a position of power over other prisoners (see Genesis 39:20–23). Using his God-given talent of interpreting dreams, he was able to gain the favor of another prisoner, the pharaoh's butler, who promised to remember Joseph when he was released from prison. But the butler forgot and Joseph lingered in prison for two more years.

5. Joseph lost his job and his freedom because of someone else's dishonesty. In your professional life, have you ever suffered an injustice because of someone else's mistake or deception? How did that incident make you feel? How are you encouraged by Joseph's response to his unfair treatment?

6. Joseph sat in a prison cell for over two years of his life, seemingly wasting his God-given talents. Have you ever felt stuck in a job that was going nowhere? That your talents and ambitions were wasting away? Read 1 Corinthians 10:31. How does this verse dictate how we are to respond to a situation in which we feel stuck?

Soon, God placed Joseph before Pharaoh and allowed him to interpret Pharaoh's dream. As a result, Joseph became one of the most influential men in Egypt, second only to Pharaoh. Joseph had power and authority over a dominant nation, and he was only thirty years old. Several years later, Joseph's brothers surfaced in Egypt, requesting food from the powerful official they did not recognize as the scrawny little brother they sold into slavery years ago. In a supreme position of authority, Joseph could have easily had his revenge. Instead, he chose to show extreme kindness to these dishonest brothers and they were humbled by his grace toward them.

7. When we find ourselves placed in positions of power over others, it's easy to feel a sense of entitlement and to exert our power in ways that can demean and dishearten those working for us. What does Romans 12:3–5 have to say about godly leadership?

8. Read Romans 13:7–8. How does this passage speak to your professional life today?

DIGGING DEEPER

It's time to take inventory of your professional life. How is the integrity of your work? Do you strive to do your best always, remembering that you are working for the Lord and not for man? If you are feeling discouraged or unappreciated in your work, be mindful of your attitude in this time of perseverance. How can you use this seemingly useless time to develop your talents and become a better worker and a stronger person? Finally, evaluate your treatment of those who work under your supervision. Are you using your position to develop and encourage others, or are you all too happy to exert your position of power?

PONDER & PRAY

This week, pray for integrity in your work and in your relationships with coworkers and with those in positions of authority. Pray that God would reveal to you areas in which you are relying on your own power instead of His. Pray for protection against bitterness and apathy in times when your perseverance is tested. Pray that you will realize that God has a grand plan for your life and that He will give you patience to wait as it unfolds. Pray that you would be kind and gracious to those entrusted to your professional care.

TRINKETS TO TREASURE

Our trinket this week is a business card, to help remind us of all the gifts that God has entrusted to us in our professional life. As Swiss philosopher Henri Frederic Amiel once stated, "Work while you have the light. You are responsible for the talent that has been entrusted to you." This week, spend some time considering whether you are being wise with what you have been given. If you need help, consider the words of James 1:5: "If any of you lacks wisdom, he should ask God, who gives generously to all without finding fault, and it will be given to him" (NIV).

CHAPTER FOUR

DOMESTIC STRENGTH

BUT AS FOR ME AND MY HOUSE, WE WILL SERVE THE LORD.

Joshua 24:15

One picture is worth ten thousand words, or so the old Chinese proverb goes. It applies not only to the two-dimensional medium of photography, but also to the three-dimensional world of your home. Through your choices of furniture and art you make a statement about your values and beliefs, what you hold dear and what you think is important. The atmosphere of your home communicates your lifestyle immediately and concisely. Ultimately, a woman's home is one of her sacred spaces.

Consider your house or apartment for a minute. Do you enjoy spending time there, or do you feel overworked and overwhelmed there? Is your home quiet and relaxing, boisterous and exciting, or talkative and nurturing? Do you feel you manage your home well, or is it out of your control? What would you change about your home?

Now think about the activities that take place in your home. Some women are homebodies, venturing out only for errands and work. Others

CLEARING ↗ THE ↖ COBWEBS

The atmosphere of your home communicates your lifestyle immediately and concisely.

are social butterflies, out and about as much as possible with very little time spent in their house. And still others combine the two, with frequent entertaining and guests at their abode weekly, if not daily. But being the constant hostess does not necessarily mean that domestic life is your strength, and being an unorganized semi-recluse doesn't mean that your family life is a failure. There are shades and aspects of hospitality and domesticity, and each of us fall somewhere in that spectrum. The sign of real strength is being able to embrace your place on the spectrum and fine-tune it to fit your purpose.

1. The story of Mary and Martha is probably the most famous story of domesticity in the Bible. Martha was the consummate party-giver, busying herself with the details of entertaining guests. Mary was an exquisite hostess as well, focusing on the purpose of hospitality. Read Luke 10:38–42. List the strengths of each woman as you imagine this scene in your head.

Mary   Martha

_____   _____

_____   _____

_____   _____

_____   _____

2. Proverbs 31 describes "the virtuous wife," a woman who is able to do it all for herself and her family and to do it effortlessly, or so it seems. List some of the characteristics of this woman in the space provided. In your opinion, what era of modern history does she seem most likely to fit into — the stay-at-home wife of the 50s, the women's libber of the 60s, or maybe the have-it-all woman of today?

3. If a complete stranger were to walk into your home, what would they know about you based only on what they see? What do the following scriptures say about home life?

Proverbs 3:33

1 Peter 4:9

Deuteronomy 11:19

Joshua 24:15

Psalm 101:7

If you feel more comfortable at the office or a party than at home, domestic tasks may not be your strength. But that doesn't mean that your home life is necessarily weak. God's design for you may be to travel and share His love with others around the world. Look at the life of Paul— he was constantly on the road. "If he spent more than one week in the same place, it was probably a prison," Max Lucado points out in *Cast of*

Characters.[1] But who would claim that Paul failed to fulfill God's call on his life?

For those of us without an interior-designing bone in our body, those who hate to host parties or tend to be messier than normal, it's reassuring to know that "home" has a number of different definitions. Not only is it the literal place where we live, but it's also the feeling we get when we're comfortable and vulnerable with someone we love. We say "it feels like home" to be with them. And, more importantly, God promises us a destination on the other side of this life—a place where all of our desires and dreams are fulfilled in Christ. Isn't it comforting to know that He calls heaven "home"?

4. How does Jesus describe His father's house in John 14:1–3? What does He promise to do for us?

5. Read Revelation 21, John 14:23, and Psalm 84:10. Why should we look forward to spending time in our eternal home?

1 Max Lucado, *Cast of Characters* (Nashville, TN: Thomas Nelson, 2008) 99.

6. How should the concept of "home" extend beyond your literal house and into your relationships and experience with Christ?

> There are shades and aspects of hospitality and domesticity, and each of us fall somewhere in that spectrum. The sign of real strength is being able to embrace your place on the spectrum and fine-tune it to fit your purpose.

7. Consider the times and places where you feel most "at home." How is Jesus ministering to you there?

DIGGING DEEPER

Take a few moments to examine your home life. Is it too rushed? Too isolated? Too messy? Too clean? Too tense? Too exciting? Write down three practical things you can do to improve one aspect of your home life and do them this week. (For example, if you're too rushed, perhaps you should eat dinner at home every night, shut off your laptop no later than ten o'clock, and take a long shower or bubble bath.)

PONDER & PRAY

If you have a home—whether you rent or own—then God has blessed you with riches and abundance many in the world don't have. Be thankful for the gift of a safe, secure home to live in. And ask God how you can use that blessing to honor Him. Consider hosting a prayer night once a month, inviting an unwed mother to live with you until her baby is born, or cooking dinners for people in your community who need the help.

TRINKETS TO TREASURE

Our trinket this week is a welcome mat, to help us consider whether we are truly welcoming the presence of God into our homes. Think week, think about ways you can dedicate your house to the Lord. Maybe you could find a beautiful scripture print to hang on the wall. Perhaps you could write a verse on the sub-flooring when you replace the carpet. Or you might choose to greet your guests with a word of promise from the Bible as they enter your house. Choose one way to make your faith a central part of your home life.

CHAPTER FIVE

PERSONAL STRENGTH

VINDICATE ME, O LORD, FOR I HAVE WALKED IN MY INTEGRITY. I HAVE ALSO TRUSTED IN THE LORD; I SHALL NOT SLIP.

Psalm 26:1

*I*magine what it must have been like for Mary, Jesus's mother. She was a young girl; most scholars suggest she was only thirteen. Her parents had arranged a good marriage for her to a nice Jewish man. She was set for a good life. She could raise children, make friends, and have a normal, happy life. But then the angel came.

She was scared at first, but who wouldn't be? And then he told her the message that would change her life forever: "You are with child." Can you imagine the thoughts that probably raced through her head? *I must be crazy. This is a dream. It's not happening, not to me. . . . He'll divorce me. He might kill me. My parents will disown me. How will I survive? And with a child to raise too?*

But "do not fear," is what he told her; it was "good news of great joy." Even though Mary couldn't comprehend the impact this would have on her life at that moment and forever, she was able to set aside her wishes and plans and trust in

CLEARING ⚹ THE ⚹ COBWEBS

Ultimately when it comes to personal strength, the greatest challenge is consistency. Any of us can be kind one moment or firm another, but for us to let our character be marked by our integrity is the work of a lifetime.

the Lord. This young girl had real strength, authentic faith in the God who had chosen her. She dug down deep into her soul and found the courage to believe God's word for her life.

1. What does Luke 1:46–55 tell us about Mary's response to her calling?

2. What experiences in your life have you had to rely on personal strength to face unexpected turns on the road of life?

3. Do you ever feel weak in your faith? Unable to stand strong against the temptations of this world? How does Psalm 41:12 reassure us in our weakness?

4. What does Proverbs 20:7 say is the reward for a life of integrity?

We've all witnessed women with incredible personal strength. It might be determination in the eyes of a cancer patient or unending patience in the heart of a mother to triplets. It might be the hard work ethic of an executive who is on the brink of winning or losing her biggest client or the gentle voice of a counselor who's guided many through the dark valleys of their lives. But where does their strength come from?

5. What does Psalm 121:2 say about the source of our strength?

Saint Francis de Sales once wrote, "There is nothing so strong as gentleness. Nothing is so gentle as real strength." When you examine your life, where do your strengths lie? Where are you gentle? How do those areas overlap or intersect? When you see them start to merge together and become unified, that's where your personal strength lies. Perhaps you're a strict mother, gently and clearly stating your expectations and staying firm in the follow-through. Or maybe you have a very compassionate bedside manner, with a quiet strength that helps carry the burdens of the weak.

Ultimately when it comes to personal strength, the greatest challenge is consistency. Any of us can be kind one moment or firm another, but for us to let our character be marked by our integrity is the work of a lifetime.

6. How does Psalm 78:72 suggest we maintain integrity over a lifetime?

7. Do you live with the fear that you'll be discovered — that your secret sins will be exposed and the world will know your failures? What does Proverbs 10:9 say in response to that fear?

8. Job was a man of faith, yet disaster entered his life in tragic proportions. Satan was trying him to see if he would abandon his faith, if he would "curse God and die" as his wife recommended. But Job, though not perfect, did maintain his trust in God. He was angry, hurt, and frustrated with his situation, but he ultimately called on God to give him understanding. And throughout his story the word "integrity" is repeated again and again. Look up the following verses and note what they each have to say about personal strength.

Job 2:3

Job 27:5

Job 4:6

Job 31:6

9. Read Job 42:3–6. What did Job ultimately realize about his own integrity or strength in light of God's strength? How is this true for all of us?

Digging Deeper

Think about your weak point, that place where you most easily collapse in your faith. Is it an inability to resist online shopping? Is it a quick temper with your husband or friends? Is it anger toward God at the thought of a terminally ill child? Strengthen yourself through prayer and study of Scripture, then face your weakness and overcome it. Every small victory will add up so that you eventually don't even recognize that temptation's power over you any longer.

Ponder & Pray

Be open to the Spirit of God this week. As we discuss personal strength, we are getting into intimate issues that are at the very core of who you are. Listen to what God is telling you in that space. Don't be afraid to follow His voice.

Trinkets to Treasure

Our trinket this week is a metronome, to help us remember to maintain a consistent rhythm in our lives when it comes to developing our talents and gifts. This week, get together with a close friend and consider what are your greatest personal strengths. How you can use those strengths on a more consistent basis? What opportunities you can pursue to help develop those qualities. Be open to where you feel God is leading you to act.

CHAPTER SIX

UNWANTED STRENGTH

BUT INDEED FOR THIS PURPOSE I HAVE RAISED YOU UP, THAT I MAY SHOW MY POWER IN YOU, AND THAT MY NAME MAY BE DECLARED IN ALL THE EARTH.

Exodus 9:16

Miss Lindsey is a preschool teacher. The children in her class adore her; they wake up on school days excitedly chanting "Miss Lindsey, Miss Lindsey" as they get dressed and climb into their minivans. She cheerfully leads them in song and story time, patiently attends to cuts and bumps, and judiciously breaks up arguments over trucks or Nilla Wafers. At the end of each day she kisses each boy or girl on the forehead, gives their parents a detailed account of the day, and wishes them a good evening at home.

The only problem is, Miss Lindsey hates her job. She feels lonely and frustrated. She thinks the children are precious, but she'd rather spend eight hours a day with adults, challenging herself intellectually.

Have you ever been really good at something that you really hate? You organize office birthday parties that are legendary but you resent doing it

CLEARING ↗ THE ↖ COBWEBS

A strength is not the same thing as a calling. And being good at something you dislike doesn't mean that you have to do it all the time.

every time. Or maybe you have an instinct that kicks in and gives you exactly the right words to say in a difficult situation but you don't like the sadness or strained relationship that can come with it.

A strength is not the same thing as a calling. And being good at something you dislike doesn't mean that you have to do it all the time. Perhaps Lindsey should volunteer once a week in the church nursery, or maybe you could alternate hosting the birthday parties. The fact is God gave you that strength for a reason, so it's worth examining yourself to see what is the best way you can use your gifts for His glory.

1. In light of Ecclesiastes 3:17, describe the way your life may go through phases — how specific work or tasks may be appropriate for you at certain times of life and different ones at other times.

2. According to Ephesians 4:1–6, what is the one calling all Christians are responsible to?

3. The answer to the Westminster shorter catechism says that our purpose is "to glorify God and enjoy him forever." In what way does your life reflect that? How do your strengths tie into this urging?

So often in the day-to-day of living we find that our focus narrows. Our thoughts are directed toward the little things that must be done in our own lives—filling up the gas tank, setting out the meat to thaw, finding an acceptable birthday present, getting an outfit just right for that event—that all we see is ourselves and our own needs. We find ourselves ignoring the warning signs that we're not fulfilling our purpose, and we coast in "get through today" mode.

Tomorrow we'll read that book we've been longing to read. Tomorrow we'll see about getting involved in that fellowship group. Tomorrow we'll sit down and really think about what it is we want to do with our lives. But meanwhile we find ourselves frustrated or bored today. It's unavoidable that we'll long for more while we live here in the shadows of heaven, but our strengths should bring us joy as we serve God gladly. It takes some time and thought to redirect our lives away from responding to the demands of everyday life and into the path of purposely living lives in which we feel fulfilled and satisfied.

4. If you could do anything for one day, what would it be? Do you have a secret wish for your life that you would love to accomplish? What does Psalm 20:4–5 say about our desires? Should you give yours more consideration than you currently do?

5. Read 1 Corinthians 7:17–24. Is it necessary for you to completely change your life to fulfill your purpose in glorifying God? How can you use your strengths in your current situation?

6. Why do you think we may be good at things we don't enjoy?

7. Is it possible to find happiness in work that's unsatisfying?

8. How does contentedness in your gifts apply to relational or emotional strengths as well?

Digging Deeper

Spend some time in thought about your personal strengths. List them on a piece of paper, or here in this study guide, and rank them in order of your favorite things to do to your least favorite. Recognizing your strengths, even those that you don't find a lot of satisfaction in, is a good start to living contentedly.

PONDER & PRAY

This week pray about the parts of your life that you find most frustrating and annoying. In what ways are you using your strengths there and in what ways are you relying more on weaknesses to get you through? Ask God to show you new strategies for accomplishing those tasks in your life, strategies that use your strengths. And ask Him to give you contentment and fulfillment in all the duties of your daily life.

TRINKETS TO TREASURE

Our trinket this week is a magnifying glass, to help us examine our lives and determine how we can best use our gifts for the Lord's glory. This week, take note of something you don't enjoy doing, but are quite good at, and spend some time "putting it under the magnifying glass." Journal your responses to these questions: *What did I dislike about this task? In what ways is this a strength for me? Is there any way to find satisfaction in this task? Should I continue to do it or delegate it to someone else?* Spend time praying for God's guidance on your decision.

CHAPTER SEVEN

STRENGTH IN WEAKNESS

AND HE SAID TO ME, "MY GRACE IS
SUFFICIENT FOR YOU, FOR MY STRENGTH
IS MADE PERFECT IN WEAKNESS."

2 Corinthians 12:9

The Oxford English Dictionary defines weakness as "the state or condition of lacking strength," a quality that is considered a fault. But how does God view human weakness? He doesn't shudder and fume when He sees us stumbling through life or struggling to make good decisions. To understand His perspective we need to take a step back from ours.

Spend some time with a toddler and you'll see this very clearly. A three-year-old has no understanding of the world apart from himself. He literally cannot comprehend outside his own experience. But we get stuck in this mind-set as well, most often when it comes to our weaknesses. We're so hard on ourselves, thinking we don't measure up and finding all the ways we've failed. And soon it becomes all we see or think about.

Remember that we all have fallen short of God's glory. If you do, you may start to see a ray of hope break through the dark clouds of

CLEARING ↗ THE ↖ COBWEBS

Weakness is not something we should be ashamed of or try to hide. Instead we should imagine ourselves as God describes us so often—as lambs in the shepherd's arms.

self-condemnation. For if we did not need saving, God would be useless. But when we are weak, helpless to save ourselves, and desperate for His spirit to invade our lives, then His glory is magnified in us. We must take an honest assessment of ourselves and see our need for a Savior, only then can He enter our lives in bold and dramatic ways, empowering us to be His strength in the world.

1. Do you fear weakness or are you ashamed of it? How does Paul describe the weaker members in our community in 1 Corinthians 12:22?

2. It is inevitable that weakness will dominate our lives at some point? Maybe it could manifest itself in a joyful but draining time after a new baby has entered your life, a fearful and anxious time after the doctor has said "malignant," or a lonely and sad time after you've sent a loved one to eternity before you. When you are at your lowest point, what do the following verses remind us to hold on to as our strength?

Matthew 26:41 and Mark 14:38

1 Corinthians 2:2–5

Hebrews 4:15

3. How does God provide for us in our weakness, according to Romans 8:26? What does this mean to you?

4. Read Acts 20:35, Romans 14:1, Romans 15:1, 1 Thessalonians 5:14. How are we to respond to those who are weak?

Each one of us is at a different place in our relationships with God, and many of us seem to vary even hour to hour in our intimacy with Him. We struggle to determine God's will in some things while others are black and white. This can create interesting dynamics in friendships and family, can't it? We may feel completely okay with an activity or relationship and others close to us may criticize our choices. Or the opposite could be true, and you could be appalled at someone's behavior who claims to be a child of God.

This reminds us of the famous and somewhat confusing "meat" discussion in 1 Corinthians. Some Christians felt free to eat meat that had been sacrificed to idols. In their minds it was going to waste and they might as well eat the meat instead of throw it out—it's not like they were going to worship the idols. Others were offended—how dare you eat something that has been contaminated by pagan religious practices? And Paul was called in to referee.

5. Read 1 Corinthians 8. What is Paul's first word of warning in this debate? Why does he start by talking about knowledge instead of the real issue?

6. What is Paul's warning to the strong in 1 Corinthians 8:9?

7. How do you see this debate in your life and faith community? What are specific things people argue about in your church community?

Emotional pain and distress are exhausting and can test anyone's faith. It's inevitable that we find ourselves weak and needing the support of others when tragedy, confusion, or overwhelming emotion of any kind enters our lives. Weakness is not something we should be ashamed of or try to hide. Instead we should imagine ourselves as God describes us so often—as lambs in the shepherd's arms.

8. Throughout the entire Bible, weak people have relied on God for their strength. Match the person with their weakness.

PERSON	WEAKNESS
Sarah	Terrible reputation as the town prostitute
Joseph	Too ignorant to recognize conniving son
Moses	Thought she was too old to have a child
Rahab	Lied about his marital status out of fear
Isaac	"Orphaned" when his mother set him adrift on the Nile River
Abraham	Hated and bullied by his brothers

9. What does Hebrews 11 have to say about each of these people? In what ways does that comfort you in your weakness?

DIGGING DEEPER

When you are weak, you are tired and run down, and the last thing you need to do is to work on improving yourself. So this week we're going to take a rest. Instead of trying to do it all and make everyone happy, take some time to relax and enjoy the gifts and support God has given you. When you feel the temptation to do too much, remind yourself to cease striving and rest in your salvation.

PONDER & PRAY

When you are at your very lowest point emotionally, physically, or mentally, it can be dark, difficult, and exhausting to pray. Sometimes all we can do is say, "Lord, I am Yours. Allow me to see Your grace in my life." And then we trust.

TRINKETS TO TREASURE

Our trinket this week is a shepherd's cane, to remind us that even though we may be weak and confused like a flock of sheep, God is always strong— and He uses us to help others. This week, think of someone you know who is weak and in need of support. If you don't know anyone personally, seek someone out through your church or a local charity. Find one way to help someone else—financially, emotionally, practically, or logistically.

NOTES & PRAYER REQUESTS

CHAPTER EIGHT

DIVINE STRENGTH

THE SOVEREIGN LORD IS MY STRENGTH.

Habakkuk 3:19 NIV

Nurse. Chef. Chauffer. Vet. Social director. Counselor. Logistics Manager. Interior designer. Maid. Daughter. Sister. Mother. Significant other. How many different roles are you expected to fulfill in a given day? Probably at least this many and more. We live in a society that tells us not only that we can do it all, but that we should. This is empowering, but it can also be overwhelming.

Throughout Scripture God consistently tells us to rely on Him for our strength. We are promised that if we drink from His well we will never be thirsty again (John 4). He tells us that He is our rock and our stronghold (Psalm 18:2).

Pay attention as you experience each day: Are your tasks truly serving God and others, or are they simply vain, striving for a bigger, better life? If you find that you are relying on your own strengths, and not God's, to accomplish all the things you have on your to-do list, it might be time to reconsider your priorities.

CLEARING ⚹ THE ⚹ COBWEBS

If you find that you are relying on your own strengths, and not God's, to accomplish all the things you have on your to-do list, it might be time to reconsider your priorities.

1. How often do you feel overwhelmed? How often do you feel inspired and motivated? Do you feel these proportions are right for your life?

2. When you feel discouraged by your to-do list and overwhelmed by life's demands, how does Habakkuk 3:19 encourage you to draw on Christ's strength?

3. According to 2 Samuel 22:33, God gives us His strength and what happens?

We're conditioned to want the *best* of everything—the best schools, the safest cars, the newest gadgets, the most powerful job, the most handsome husband. But we don't need top-of-the-line everything. The truth is that sometimes "just okay" is actually the best for us. We learn to live contentedly, simply.

When we strive for perfection on our own terms we find ourselves frustrated because there's no way we can do it all! But if we recognize our limitations and call on the Lord, He will give us peace and satisfaction. Our culture has groomed us to think that more working and rushing equals more success, which equals "the best," which equals happiness. But God calls on us to rest and let Him do for us what we wouldn't even dream of for ourselves.

4. We *need* God to survive. He's not just the "sugar on top." He's the essence of life, the Living Water, the Bread of Life. What promise does the psalmist give us in Psalm 73:26?

5. Read 2 Corinthians 12:9. How does recognizing that God supplies our every need free us to enjoy life?

6. How has God provided you strength in the last year? What specific event or conversation caused you to seek His sustenance for your daily life? What did that look like? (For example, more time in prayer? A willingness to let another person step in and help? Peace flooding your spirit?)

When we live lives that draw from the strength of God rather than from our own limited human strength, we are calm, focused, and intentional with our choices. Isn't that what we all long for—respite from the rushing and the working? And relying on God allows us to recognize the opportunities He gives us to speak His strength into the lives of others.

7. What does Isaiah 12:2–5 have to say about sharing God's strength?

DIGGING DEEPER

Take a few minutes to examine your life. What are you struggling to accomplish today? What do you have to do that you hate or resent doing? How can you draw on God's divine strength to fulfill that obligation? Identify one practical thing you can do to rely on God more.

PONDER & PRAY

As you pray this week, ask God to turn your heart toward Him in all things. Ask Him to show you His strength in your life and to help you see those places where you're grasping for control. Tell Him you trust Him to provide for all your needs. Prayerfully speak aloud some of the verses you read in this chapter.

TRINKETS TO TREASURE

Our trinket this week is a lounge chair, to remind us to spend time resting in the Lord's strength. This week, look over your schedule and examine it closely. Are all of your activities necessary? Is there anything you could eliminate? Be intentional about planning time to rest. Honor that time commitment the same way you would honor lunch with a girlfriend or a meeting with your boss.

NOTES & PRAYER REQUESTS

CHAPTER NINE

BUILDING STRENGTH

HE WHO HAS BEGUN A GOOD WORK IN YOU WILL COMPLETE IT UNTIL THE DAY OF JESUS CHRIST.

Philippians 1:6

You probably have a pretty good idea of what your strengths are by now. Perhaps you have a very calm, nurturing spirit and work really well with people. Or maybe you prefer to work alone, creating art or analyzing numbers, doing your work quietly and to the glory of God. You know that some things in your life are just second nature; they happen without you having to think about them.

The places in your life when you're happy with your accomplishments and you feel satisfied with the end result—those are your strengths. If you identify them in your life, paying attention to your spirit's response to your everyday activities, you'll be able to live with purpose and poise. You'll feel the freedom to utilize your gifts and delegate where you don't have strengths. But we shouldn't stop there. We should always be seeking new ways to honor and glorify God with our lives, and when we find new talents we find new opportunities to encourage and inspire even more people to worship Christ.

CLEARING ↗ THE ↖ COBWEBS

We should always be seeking new ways to honor and glorify God with our lives, and if we find new talents we may find more opportunities to encourage and inspire even more people to worship Christ.

1. In what area have you always desired to be skilled but find yourself lacking natural talent?

2. How might learning a new skill give you opportunity to share Christ with others?

Perhaps the reason many of your strengths come so easily to you is because those are the places where God is working through you, moving your hands or eyes or mouth or feet or mind for His glory. You have truly become a vessel for His glory, allowing Him to use you to change the world!

But don't leave it at that. We find it easy to say, "Oh, I'm actually not that good at managing people" or "I'd love to help coordinate that party; I'm really organized!" Don't pigeonhole yourself by your strengths. The Scriptures tell us to grow in wisdom, to be diligent in our faith. These are instructions to work, to build, and to improve ourselves daily until the time we reach heaven and are perfected eternally for His glory.

3. All we do should be for God's approval, not for other people's approval. But when it comes to our skills and strengths it is easy to seek praise from our friends, family, and coworkers. How does 2 Timothy 2:15 suggest we gain God's favor?

4. According to Galatians 6:9, what will happen if we persevere in doing good things for the Lord?

5. What do the following Proverbs say will happen to a lazy woman, one who ignores the work and call of God in her life?

Proverbs 12:24

Proverbs 12:27

Proverbs 13:4

Proverbs 19:24

Proverbs 20:4

Proverbs 21:25

The body of Christ is made up of many people, all with unique gifts and strengths. And when we all work in unity we are able to bring glory to God. But where there is dissention and a struggle for control and power, God's work is not accomplished.

6. Read Ephesians 4:14–16. What is the benefit to society and community when everyone is diligent to perform his or her strengths for the good of the group?

7. What new activity will you try this week?

DIGGING DEEPER

What is the one area you most want to work on developing in your personality, your skill set, or your lifestyle? Write it down and put the note somewhere where you will see it every day. Each time you see that note, evaluate where you are in your development. The constant reminder will be a good motivator for growth.

PONDER & PRAY

Ask God to show you a hidden strength. You may not realize that you're very good at something, and God may be desiring to give you opportunities to use that gift. Prayerfully consider requests on your time and resources—could this be God giving you a chance to glorify Him in a new way? Maybe; maybe not. Each case will be different, which is why you should take each one to Him.

TRINKETS TO TREASURE

Our trinket this week is a dumbbell weight, to remind us to continually look for ways "exercise" our talents and abilities. This week, sign up for a class or ask someone to teach you a new skill. Learning something new will equip you to serve others better, expand your horizons, and help you meet people outside your normal social circle.

NOTES & PRAYER REQUESTS

_____

_____

_____

_____

_____

_____

_____

_____

_____

_____

_____

_____

_____

_____

_____

_____

_____

_____

_____

_____

_____

_____

Embracing Strength

The Lord gives strength to his people.

Psalm 29:11 NIV

At some point during our crucial growing-up years, all of us have looked in the mirror and not liked what we saw. Maybe it was a painfully shy girl who didn't get asked to the prom. Or the peppy cheerleader who no one took seriously. Or the bookworm who would rather study than socialize. Or the tomboy who didn't seem to fit in anywhere.

Too often we carry these old insecurities and fears into our adult lives as well, distorting the truth about who we are and what we were created to be. It takes time—along with a lot of prayer, encouragement, and a big dose of courage—to be able to look past those insecurities and fears and to learn to celebrate how God has made each of us. Before we can embrace the strength and courage God offers us, we must get rid of our old perceptions and see what Scripture has to tell us about who we are in God's eyes.

Clearing ⚹ the ⚹ Cobwebs

Before we can embrace the strength and courage God offers us, we must get rid of our old perceptions and see what Scripture has to tell us about who we are in God's eyes.

1. Has there ever been a time in your life when you were unhappy with yourself, when you felt "less than," when you didn't fit in? Why do you think you were dissatisfied or discouraged with yourself at that time?

2. What does Romans 8:15–17 tell you about who you are in God's eyes?

3. Because God recognizes us as His children, and the Holy Spirit dwells in us as believers, we are gifted with all of the fruits of the Spirit described in Galatians 5:22–23: love, joy, peace, patience, kindness, goodness, faithfulness, gentleness, and self-control.

4. Have you ever considered that these are gifts you have already been given? How does that idea change your perspective on these attributes? What else have we been given, according to Psalm 29:11?

So what does all this mean? It means no more hiding in the shadows, bullied by your own fears, insecurities, and inabilities. It means you can boldly face any challenge that comes your way in life, in the full confidence that you cannot handle everything on your own.

You are a child of God, and He has made all His resources available to you! Do you need love for a frustrating coworker? God offers you the ability to claim that love and act on it. Need patience for dealing with an unruly child? All you have to do is ask. Just as a loving and wise parent would withhold no good thing from her child, so God does not hold back from us. And so we cling to His promises—that we are heirs to His power and might.

Too often we live powerless lives, forgetting to tap into the power and the strength that God gives us so freely. Drawing on God's strength to live our lives means that we have the power to accept who we are, celebrate our strengths, and walk confidently in the knowledge that God will finish the good work He began in us (see Philippians 1:6).

5. Throughout Scripture, we are given examples of people who claimed God's strength in their lives and were therefore able to accomplish extraordinary things. Read each Scripture below and identify the person and the action that he or she took. Which character's situation resonates most with you and why?

Scripture	Person	Action
1 Samuel 25	_____	_____
1 Samuel 17:45–50	_____	_____
Joshua 2	_____	_____
Esther 5:1–8; 7:1–5	_____	_____

6. Consider Jesus's words to the disciples in Matthew 17:19–20. How do these words speak to your life? Do they inspire you, challenge you, or comfort you?

7. God has a unique purpose for your life, and He has created you — His child — with countless unique abilities to use and enjoy. What do you think keeps you from fully embracing your unique strengths and confidently using them?

8. In what specific areas of your life is God calling you out of the shadows of your own insecurities and fears and into His light? Where is He calling you to claim His strength and power in your life?

DIGGING DEEPER

Take some time this week to meditate on your status as a child of God. How might fully embracing this heavenly heritage change your perspective? Your attitude? Your relationships? Your work? Your service? Meditate on Psalm 29:11: "The Lord gives strength to his people" (NIV). Think of at least one specific way in which you can claim His strength in your life this week.

PONDER & PRAY

In your prayer time this week, ask God to help you see yourself through His eyes. Pray that you can rest in the knowledge that He has claimed you as His own, and that because of your treasured role, you can confidently face any situation or circumstance that comes your way. Pray that you would recognize the unique gifts that you have been given and that you would use them for God's glory.

TRINKETS TO TREASURE

Our trinket this week is a flashlight, to remind us to draw on God's light to help us see past our old insecurities, fears, inabilities, and self-doubt. This week, reflect on 2 Corinthians 5:17: "If anyone is in Christ, the new creation has come: The old has gone, the new is here!" (NIV). How does this verse encourage you as you reflect on what God has done for you? How does it encourage you as you reflect on what it means to be claimed and transformed by Him?

NOTES & PRAYER REQUESTS

_____

_____

_____

_____

_____

_____

_____

_____

_____

CHAPTER ELEVEN

CELEBRATING STRENGTH

I WILL PRAISE YOU, FOR I AM FEARFULLY
AND WONDERFULLY MADE.

Psalm 139:14

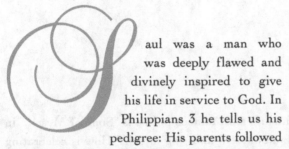

*S*aul was a man who was deeply flawed and divinely inspired to give his life in service to God. In Philippians 3 he tells us his pedigree: His parents followed all religious customs; his family tree goes deep into the roots of Israel, part of the most legalistic, upright branches of Judaism. But apart from Christ he was an absolute failure—his greatest fame was his persecution of the Christian church. But when Christ got a hold of his life and redirected all his efforts, Saul became Paul, one of the most beloved and respected Christians of all times. Why? Because he celebrated his strengths.

He knew exactly who God had called him to be—an apostle of the gospel of Christ. His entire life fit into that paradigm. "Yet indeed I also count all things loss for the excellence of the knowledge of Christ Jesus my Lord, for whom I have suffered the loss of all things, and count them as rubbish, that I may gain Christ and be found in

CLEARING ↗ THE ↖ COBWEBS

When we use our gifts and talents in service of him, sacrificially giving of our time and resources to further God's influence on another's life, we are celebrating our strengths.

Him" (Philippians 3:8–9). He wanted nothing but to know Christ and serve him. His calling was his only joy. Nothing else would satisfy. And he wanted all men to know of the love that had changed his life eternally.

1. Does your life match the description of Paul's? Is there anything you should change about your daily habits to serve Christ better?

2. One of Walt Whitman's most famous poems is "Song of Myself," in which he says, "I celebrate myself, and sing myself." How is celebrating your strengths different from this idea?

3. Scripture repeatedly tells us to enjoy God and His gifts. Why is this?

4. Match the Scripture reference with the gift below.

SCRIPTURE	GIFT
Joshua 1:15	The work of your hands
2 Chronicles 36:21	The good in labor
Ecclesiastes 2:24	The land
Isaiah 65:22	All things
Romans 15:24	Sabbaths

We all have our own personal preference when it comes to sharing the gospel with others. You may be comfortable speaking directly about the good work Christ has done in your life. Or you may prefer to let your actions speak louder than words, hesitant to speak prematurely into the life of an unbeliever. Whatever your style, we are all called to take the gospel to the ends of the earth. And one way God equips us to do this is through our strengths.

When we use our gifts and talents in service of Him, sacrificially giving of our time and resources to further God's influence on another's life, we are celebrating our strengths.

5. How can you apply Matthew 28:19–20 in your own life in a way that fits well with the strengths God has given you?

6. What is your personal evangelism style? How do you most often share God's love with others? Are you willing to try a new method or strategy in your relationships?

7. Take ten minutes to brainstorm the following question: In what way is God calling you to celebrate your strengths in your home and family, your church, your community? Give practical and specific answers.

DIGGING DEEPER

If you're the type who likes to quietly share your faith, get out of your comfort zone by speaking boldly about Christ's love for you and how he's blessed you and equipped you for every good work (Hebrews 13:20–21). If you're more comfortable talking about your faith, take a minute to just listen to someone struggling with faith.

PONDER & PRAY

Ask God to show you ways to celebrate His blessings in your life this week. Look for new ways to use your strengths, and as you do be sure to acknowledge God's gifts to you.

TRINKETS TO TREASURE

Our trinket this week is a megaphone, to remind us how our strengths can broadcast the gospel to the world. Look for ways this week to share what God has done for you. You can choose to share your story of God's grace with others, or you can demonstrate God's love in others ways by making a meal for someone or doing chores for someone in need. There are many ways to be the hands and feet of the Lord, so look for a creative way to announce the gospel this week.

NOTES & PRAYER REQUESTS

_____

_____

_____

_____

_____

_____

_____

_____

_____

_____

CHAPTER TWELVE

WHERE DO I GO FROM HERE?

NOW MAY THE GOD OF PEACE . . . MAKE YOU COMPLETE
IN EVERY GOOD WORK TO DO HIS WILL, WORKING IN
YOU WHAT IS WELL PLEASING IN HIS SIGHT, THROUGH
JESUS CHRIST, TO WHOM BE GLORY FOREVER AND EVER.

Hebrews 13:20–21

The next step in our journeys toward becoming the women God has designed us to be—strong, secure, and sensational—is to listen to His voice speaking into our lives. He may be whispering for you to slow down and focus. Or perhaps He's asking you to make a significant and daring change in your lifestyle. One thing we can rest assured in is that He will never ask us to do something we cannot manage. How do we know this? He will always allow us to draw on His unending strength to survive any trial or face any task.

Because we have this security in Christ, we can fearlessly explore new ways to serve and glorify Him. When we try something new, we should be especially sensitive to our spirit. What is God telling us as we look for new ways to worship Him—whether it's painting, volunteering, organizing, or listening. In all things, He will speak to us. He will let us know the right way for us as

CLEARING ⟅ THE ⟆ COBWEBS

Listen for His voice to guide you win the way you should go.

individuals to honor him. So as you move forward in your journey, listen for His voice to reassure and guide you in the way you should go.

1. Do you ever take time to sit and just listen to God's voice in your life? What does He say to you in those quiet moments?

2. What do these verses say about the way we recognize and respond to God's voice in our lives?

Deuteronomy 13:4

Job 37:5

Psalm 95:6–8

Ezekiel 10:5

John 5:25

God has called many people to make bizarre and unusual demonstrations of their faith. Though they each had very understandable reasons to doubt what God was really asking them to do, they still obeyed and moved forward in faith. Taking such a dramatic step of faith can cause you to doubt: What will people think? Is this really God's voice in my life? How will I know if I'm doing the right thing? How will I explain this choice? Why would God ask me to do something so unusual and against the norm?

When doubts plague your mind, take time to pray. Ask God for assurance that what you are doing brings glory to Him. Ask Him to give you wisdom as you move forward in faith. And look to the people who have gone before you and learn from their lives, their doubts, and their faith.

3. The chart below lists some of the most famous people in Christian history and their callings from God. Identify the strength that God wanted to use in them.

Person	Calling	Strength
Abraham	Leave home	_____
Esther	Save the Jews	_____
Solomon	Build the temple	_____
John the Baptist	Prepare the way for Jesus	_____
Jonah	Take the gospel to Ninevah	_____

4. Has God ever asked you to do something beyond your comfort zone? How did you know it was His voice speaking in your life? How did you respond?

5. As our study on strengths comes to a close, we should look back over what we've learned so far. What topic or verse has spoken most intimately to your spirit?

6. What is one practical thing you will do to spread the gospel by using your strengths in the next week?

7. If God calls you to use your strengths in a way you're not comfortable with, how will you respond?

DIGGING DEEPER

God uses the circumstances of life to shape us, stretch us, and perfect our faith. When an uncomfortable opportunity arises in your life, find the strength deep down to accept the challenge head on. Don't fear failure or persecution, instead think back on all of the amazing gifts God has given you for your salvation and draw strength from Him to succeed!

PONDER & PRAY

Meditate on God's goodness to you. Be quiet as you listen for his voice in your life. Sometimes it's a still, small whisper. Other times it roars like the sounds of many waters. But no matter what, God knows your deepest desires and your inner design. He will speak to the strengths He has put within you, so don't fear when you hear His voice in your spirit.

TRINKETS TO TREASURE

Our trinket this week is a pair of earbuds, to remind us to continually listen for God's voice in our lives. This week, share what you've learned about yourself with one other person, and ask him or her to keep you accountable to use your strengths to bring glory to Christ all the time, not just when it's convenient. Thank God for the things He's taught you and ask Him to lead you in the days ahead. Then be open to what you hear God saying to you!

NOTES & PRAYER REQUESTS

_____

_____

_____

_____

_____

_____

_____

_____

_____

_____

_____

_____

_____

_____

_____

_____

_____

_____

_____

_____

SHALL WE REVIEW?

Every chapter has added a new trinket to your treasure trove of memories. Let's remind ourselves of the lessons they hold for us!

1. Graduation Cap

The graduation cap helps remind us to exercise our minds. Our intellect is a precious gift from God, and we need to maintain it just as we would any other aspect of our lives.

2. A Friendship Bracelet

A friendship bracelet helps us to remember the importance of relationships in our lives. We need to understand the inner-workings of the bonds we make in order to strengthen our friendships in a way that brings glory to the Lord.

3. A Business Card

The business card reminds us to care for the gifts God has entrusted to use in our professional lives. We must consider whether we are being wise with the talents God has given to us.

4. A Welcome Mat

The welcome mat reminds us to always invite God's presence into our homes. When we choose to make our faith a central part of our home life, we bring glory to God.

5. A Metronome

Musicians use a metronome to keep a consistent rhythm when performing a piece. In the same way, we must be consistent when it comes to developing our talents and gifts.

6. A Magnifying Glass

The magnifying glass reminds us to examine ourselves to determine how we can best use our gifts for the Lord's glory. It's our responsibility to use the gifts God has given us to the best of our ability.

7. A Shepherd's Cane

The shepherd's cane reminds us of how God cares for us— "the sheep of his pasture" (Psalm 100:3 NIV)—and how we are likewise called to care for others.

8. A Lounge Chair

The lounge chair reminds us to spend some time just resting in the Lord's strength. We need to be intentional about planning times of rest and honor those commitments.

9. A Dumbbell Weight

Body-builders increase their physical strength with weights. In the same way, God calls on us to continually "exercise" and strengthen our talents and skills.

10. A Flashlight

The flashlight reminds us to draw on God's strength to see past the darkness of our old insecurities, fears, inabilities, and self-doubt.

11. A Megaphone

The megaphone reminds us that our strengths can broadcast the gospel to everyone we meet. Each of us has unique and important gifts in the body of Christ, and there are many ways we can celebrate those strengths and bring glory to the Lord.

12. Earbuds

The pair of earbuds reminds us to listen closely for the voice of God. God will use others in our lives to keep us accountable and help us follow what He is asking us to do.

LEADER'S GUIDE

Chapter 1

Focus: We know we should exercise our bodies and eat healthy foods, so we should do the same for our minds. If we let our intellect fade and numb our minds with useless things, that is what will come out of us in the form of words, ideas, or actions.

1. "The name of the man was Nabal, and the name of his wife Abigail. And she was a woman of good understanding and beautiful appearance" (1 Samuel 25:3). "Blessed be the Lord God of Israel, who made heaven and earth, for He has given King David a wise son, endowed with prudence and understanding" (2 Chronicles 2:12). "I have heard of you, that the Spirit of God is in you, and that light and understanding and excellent wisdom are found in you" (Daniel 5:14). "Who was with the proconsul, Sergius Paulus, an intelligent man. This man called for Barnabas and Saul and sought to hear the word of God" (Acts 13:7). All of these people defied the conventions of their time and followed the voice of God, seeking His will. While they were not perfect people, they sought the wisdom of the Lord above all.

2. "They do not know nor understand; For He has shut their eyes, so that they cannot see, And their hearts, so that they cannot understand" (Isaiah 44:18). "And He opened their understanding, that they might comprehend the Scriptures" (Luke 24:45). Before Jesus entered the world in all His humble majesty, we were blind to the truth of the Scriptures. We only had hope. But with Jesus's arrival He opened our eyes that we may understand the truth of the gospel. And those who seek it will have intelligence.

3. "Therefore you shall lay up these words of mine in your heart and in your soul, and bind them as a sign on your hand, and they shall be as frontlets between your eyes" (Deuteronomy 11:18). "For this is the covenant that I will make . . . says the Lord: I will put My laws in their mind and write them on their hearts; and I will be their God, and they shall be My people"

(Hebrews 8:10). In the Old Testament we are still under the law, subject to our own obedience of the command. But in the New Testament God graciously fulfills the law for us, so that we no longer have to rely on our own intelligence and memory of the law but only on His grace through faith.

4. "And do not be conformed to this world, but be transformed by the renewing of your mind, that you may prove what is that good and acceptable and perfect will of God" (Romans 12:2). Without a sharp mind, we will easily succumb to the ways of the world. But by keeping our minds focused on God, we will quickly recognize the tricks of the devil to trap us in sin.

5. "And even as they did not like to retain God in their knowledge, God gave them over to a debased mind, to do those things which are not fitting" (Romans 1:28). When we ignore God in our thoughts and fill our minds with the things of this world, we lose any concept of what is true and what is lies. As a result, we start behaving as if the lies are the truth and live corrupt and immoral lives.

6. Answers

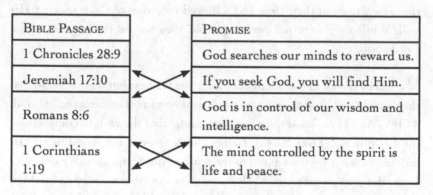

BIBLE PASSAGE	PROMISE
1 Chronicles 28:9	God searches our minds to reward us.
Jeremiah 17:10	If you seek God, you will find Him.
Romans 8:6	God is in control of our wisdom and intelligence.
1 Corinthians 1:19	The mind controlled by the spirit is life and peace.

7. "For those who are such do not serve our Lord Jesus Christ, but their own belly, and by smooth words and flattering speech deceive the hearts of the simple. For your obedience has become known to all. Therefore I am glad on your behalf; but I want you to be wise in what is good, and simple concerning evil. And the God of peace will crush Satan under your feet shortly" (Romans 16:18–20). "What is the conclusion then? I will pray with the spirit, and I will also pray with the understanding. I will sing with the spirit, and I will also sing with the understanding" (1 Corinthians 14:15). "You will keep him in perfect peace, whose mind is stayed on You" (Isaiah 26:3). "Bringing every thought into captivity to the obedience of Christ" (2 Corinthians 10:5). We must focus our minds on God and His promises alone, making our thoughts captive to obeying Him.

8. "And the peace of God, which surpasses all understanding, will guard your hearts and minds through Christ Jesus" (Philippians 4:7). If our minds are settled on Christ, we will have peace. And if we have peace, we will be fearless to change this world for good.

Chapter 2

Focus: God has given us each other to walk with in our spiritual journeys. But our friends can hurt us as well as heal, and it's important to understand our relationships to avoid creating painful emotions for those we love.

1. "He who covers a transgression seeks love, but he who repeats a matter separates friends" (Proverbs 17:9). "A friend loves at all times" (Proverbs 17:17). "A man who has friends must himself be friendly" (Proverbs 18:24). "Faithful are the wounds of a friend, but the kisses of an enemy are deceitful" (Proverbs 27:6). "The sweetness of a man's friend gives delight by hearty counsel" (Proverbs 27:9). "Do not forsake your own friend or your father's friend, nor go to your brother's house in the day of your calamity; better is a neighbor nearby than a brother far away" (Proverbs 27:10). Ultimately a friend is someone who is there for you at all times and in all ways — she is willing to speak truth into your life and to be there to support you when bad things happen. She's willing to love you unconditionally and to forgive the wounds of relationship.

2. "The righteous should choose his friends carefully, For the way of the wicked leads them astray" (Proverbs 12:26). "Do not trust in a friend; Do not put your confidence in a companion" (Micah 7:5). "Do not be deceived: 'Evil company corrupts good habits'" (1 Corinthians 15:33). While friends are one of the greatest blessings and joys in life, a bad friend can be not only emotionally damaging but spiritually damaging as well. As you get to know people, get to know their hearts and search their souls. Make sure you are in agreement on the truths of the gospel before you bind your heart to theirs in friendship. If you recognize that this new friend is not spiritually mature, use caution in your friendship and protect your heart from negative influence.

3. "However, Jesus did not permit him, but said to him, 'Go home to your friends, and tell them what great things the Lord has done for you, and how He has had compassion on you'" (Mark 5:19). In both the blessings and trials of life, God has compassion on us. When you're able to look into your life and see the compassion of God during painful times, you'll be less likely to feel anger, jealousy, or resentment toward a friend who's experiencing abundant gifts. And when you're the recipient of great things from God, you can see His mercy in your life and extend that to your friends who are suffering without gloating in your circumstances.

4. Proverbs 16:28 —— "a whisperer separates the best of friends"
Proverbs 27:6 —— "faithful are the wounds of a friend"
Proverbs 27:9 —— "the sweetness of a man's friend gives delight by hearty counsel"
Ephesians 4:15 —— "speaking the truth in love"
Hebrews 10:24 —— "stir up love and good works"
3 John 14 —— "greet the friends by name"

5. "So the Lord spoke to Moses face to face, as a man speaks to his friend" (Exodus 33:11). "A friend loves at all times, And a brother is born for adversity" (Proverbs 17:17). "For you, brethren, have been called to liberty; only do not use liberty as an opportunity for the flesh, but through love serve one another" (Galatians 5:13). If we take the time to speak with our friends face to face, rather than through e-mail or cell phones only; if we make the effort to serve our friends through love (not self-seeking or prideful efforts), then we will deepen relationships based on vulnerability and honesty.

6. Answers

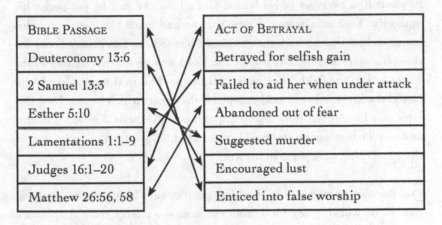

BIBLE PASSAGE		ACT OF BETRAYAL
Deuteronomy 13:6		Betrayed for selfish gain
2 Samuel 13:3		Failed to aid her when under attack
Esther 5:10		Abandoned out of fear
Lamentations 1:1–9		Suggested murder
Judges 16:1–20		Encouraged lust
Matthew 26:56, 58		Enticed into false worship

"If we are faithless, He remains faithful; He cannot deny Himself" (2 Timothy 2:13). Even though we are unfaithful friends to God, He remains faithful to us when He lives in us. We are still His friends, through grace, even when we sin against God.

7. 1 John 3:1a says, "Behold what manner of love the Father has bestowed on us, that we should be called children of God!" John 15:14 says, "You are my friends if you do whatever I command you." In this we see that we must be willing to receive God's love for us, and we must respond likewise by following His commands. He is gracious to us in our imperfection, though, as the Bible promises that God sees His son, Jesus, when He looks at us — that is, He sees perfection not failure.

Chapter 3

Focus: In our professional lives, we will always face challenges and setbacks, but if we choose to focus on them, we will miss out on the grand opportunities that also come our way.

1. Answers will vary.

2. "So Joseph found favor in [Potiphar's] sight, and served him. Then he made him overseer of his house, and all that he had he put under his authority. So it was, from the time that he had made him overseer of his house and all that he had, that the Lord blessed the Egyptian's house for Joseph's sake; and the blessing of the Lord was on all that he had in the house and in the field. Thus he left all that he had in Joseph's hand, and he did not know what he had except for the bread which he ate. Now Joseph was handsome in form and appearance" (Genesis 39:4–6). Possible answers: he was a good steward, honest, kind, diligent, efficient, trustworthy, respectful, took pride in his work.

3. Encourage members to think of specific ways in which this perspective — of working for God, and not man — affects their daily work lives. How might they act differently? How would this perspective affect the quality of their work?

4. Having this perspective would raise the bar of integrity in the workplace. Often, we can get discouraged if we dwell on the fact that we work for infallible people. We can become apathetic, paranoid, and self-serving. But if we have the perspective that we are actually working for God and His purposes, we can find a new level of peace and satisfaction in our work.

5. Answers will vary here, but it's likely that most members will feel that they have suffered some kind of injustice or discrimination in their professional lives. Be sensitive and allow members to respond, but be careful not to let these injustices take center stage — point them to Joseph's response of continued integrity, patience, and dependence on the Lord, knowing that God is the only one who can make things right. If need be, point out Romans 12:19: "Do not take revenge, my dear friends, but leave room for God's wrath, for it is written: 'It is mine to avenge; I will repay,' says the Lord" (NIV).

6. Whatever you do, do it all for the glory of God" (1 Corinthians 10:31 NIV). The key here is that we do not know God's ultimate plans for our lives, and when we experience times of feeling stuck or spinning our wheels in what appears to be a dead-end job, we should pray about it, asking God for wisdom and direction in what is to come. We should also pray that we would continue to have integrity in the work we are doing for as long as we are doing it — for God's glory, not our own.

7. "For by the grace given me I say to every one of you: Do not think of yourself more highly than you ought, but rather think of yourself with sober judgment, in accordance with the faith God has distributed to each of you. For just as each of us has one body with many members, and these members do not all have the same function, so in Christ we, though many, form one body, and each member belongs to all the others" (Romans 12:3–5 NIV). When we are placed in positions of leadership, we must remember this doesn't mean we are better than those placed under our care. A godly leader does not abuse her power, causing others to feel intimidated or demeaned, but instead strives to bring out the best in each of them, developing their skills and rewarding a job well done.

8. "Give everyone what you owe them: If you owe taxes, pay taxes; if revenue, then revenue; if respect, then respect; if honor, then honor. Let no debt remain outstanding, except the continuing debt to love one another, for whoever loves others has fulfilled the law" (Romans 13:7–8 NIV). Some possible applications: Giving respect to those in authority positions over you; having integrity in the financial affairs of your business; treating every person — no matter his or her position — with respect and dignity; striving to show God's love in your day-to-day work.

Chapter 4

Focus: There are shades and aspects of hospitality and domesticity, and each of us fall somewhere in that spectrum. The sign of real strength is being able to embrace your place on the spectrum and fine-tune it to fit your purpose.

1. "Now it happened as they went that He entered a certain village; and a certain woman named Martha welcomed Him into her house. And she had a sister called Mary, who also sat at Jesus' feet and heard His word. But Martha was distracted with much serving, and she approached Him

and said, 'Lord, do You not care that my sister has left me to serve alone? Therefore tell her to help me.' And Jesus answered and said to her, 'Martha, Martha, you are worried and troubled about many things. But one thing is needed, and Mary has chosen that good part, which will not be taken away from her'" (Luke 10:38–42). Mary's strengths include a welcoming spirit, an interest in the Scriptures, relational focus, good conversationalist, single-minded focus, and devotion. Martha's strengths include service, assertiveness, faith (she calls him "Lord," see also John 11), and a demand for excellence in all things.

2. "Who can find a virtuous wife? For her worth is far above rubies. The heart of her husband safely trusts her; So he will have no lack of gain. She does him good and not evil All the days of her life. She seeks wool and flax, And willingly works with her hands. She is like the merchant ships, She brings her food from afar. She also rises while it is yet night, And provides food for her household, And a portion for her maidservants. She considers a field and buys it; From her profits she plants a vineyard. She girds herself with strength, And strengthens her arms. She perceives that her merchandise is good, And her lamp does not go out by night. She stretches out her hands to the distaff, And her hand holds the spindle. She extends her hand to the poor, Yes, she reaches out her hands to the needy. She is not afraid of snow for her household, For all her household is clothed with scarlet. She makes tapestry for herself; Her clothing is fine linen and purple. Her husband is known in the gates, When he sits among the elders of the land. She makes linen garments and sells them, And supplies sashes for the merchants. Strength and honor are her clothing; She shall rejoice in time to come. She opens her mouth with wisdom, And on her tongue is the law of kindness. She watches over the ways of her household, And does not eat the bread of idleness. Her children rise up and call her blessed; Her husband also, and he praises her: 'Many daughters have done well, But you excel them all.' Charm is deceitful and beauty is passing, But a woman who fears the Lord, she shall be praised. Give her of the fruit of her hands, And let her own works praise her in the gates" (Proverbs 31:10–31).

3. "The curse of the Lord is on the house of the wicked, But He blesses the home of the just" (Proverbs 3:33). "Be hospitable to one another without grumbling" (1 Peter 4:9). "You shall teach them to your children, speaking of them when you sit in your house, when you walk by the way, when you lie down, and when you rise up" (Deuteronomy 11:19). "But as for me and my house, we will serve the Lord" (Joshua 24:15). "He who works deceit shall not dwell within my house; He who tells lies shall not continue in my presence" (Psalm 101:7). "He who troubles his own house will inherit the wind, And the fool will be servant to the wise of heart" (Proverbs 11:29).

4. "Let not your heart be troubled; you believe in God, believe also in Me. In My Father's house are many mansions; if it were not so, I would have told you. I go to prepare a place for you. And if I go and prepare a place for you, I will come again and receive you to Myself; that where I am, there you may be also" (John 14:1–3).

5. Our life here on earth is so filled with struggle and pain, but life in heaven will be free of that. We will not focus on ourselves at all, but we will spend our days perfectly glorifying God. That is an amazing thought.

6. When most people speak of home, they usually have fond memories of warm, cozy holidays and the love of parents and family. But others, tragically, do not. Let that spirit of love and unconditional acceptance permeate all your relationships, so that people feel that they are "at home" in your company.

7. Answers will vary.

Chapter 5

Focus: Ultimately when it comes to personal strength, the greatest challenge is consistency. Any of us can be kind one moment or firm another, but for us to let our character be marked by our integrity is the work of a lifetime.

1. "And Mary said:
   'My soul magnifies the Lord,
   And my spirit has rejoiced in God my Savior.
   For He has regarded the lowly state of His maidservant;
   For behold, henceforth all generations will call me blessed.
   For He who is mighty has done great things for me,
   And holy is His name.
   And His mercy is on those who fear Him
   From generation to generation.
   He has shown strength with His arm;
   He has scattered the proud in the imagination of their hearts.
   He has put down the mighty from their thrones,
   And exalted the lowly.
   He has filled the hungry with good things,
   And the rich He has sent away empty.
   He has helped His servant Israel,
   In remembrance of His mercy,
   As He spoke to our fathers,
   To Abraham and to his seed forever'" (Luke 1:46–55)

Mary decided to trust God in His decisions for her life, not only in her pregnancy, but in the thirty-three years she spent as Jesus's mother—raising the Son of God as a toddler, observing him as a young adult, and walking with him to his death as an adult.

2. Mary was sure to have doubts —— she was, in fact, human. But in those doubts she was willing to trust God's will. She set aside her own desires and just asked God to help her be strong.

3. "As for me, You uphold me in my integrity, And set me before Your face forever" (Psalm 41:12). God is the one who gives us strength to be faithful to His word and His command. We do not have to find that strength in ourselves.

4. "The righteous man walks in his integrity; His children are blessed after him" (Proverbs 20:7).

5. "My help comes from the Lord, who made heaven and earth" (Psalm 121:2).

6. "So he shepherded them according to the integrity of his heart, And guided them by the skillfulness of his hands" (Psalm 78:72). If we allow God to be our shepherd for a lifetime we will live with integrity.

7. "He who walks with integrity walks securely, But he who perverts his ways will become known" (Proverbs 10:9). If we don't have the strength to live faithful lives, we will be exposed. That should encourage us to be all the more diligent in our belief.

8. "Then the Lord said to Satan, 'Have you considered My servant Job, that there is none like him on the earth, a blameless and upright man, one who fears God and shuns evil? And still he holds fast to his integrity, although you incited Me against him, to destroy him without cause'" (Job 2:3). "Far be it from me That I should say you are right; Till I die I will not put away my integrity from me" (Job 27:5). "Is not your reverence your confidence? And the integrity of your ways your hope?" (Job 4:6) "Let me be weighed on honest scales, That God may know my integrity" (Job 31:6).

9. "You asked, 'Who is this who hides counsel without knowledge?' Therefore I have uttered what I did not understand, Things too wonderful for me, which I did not know. Listen, please, and let me speak; You said, 'I will question you, and you shall answer Me,' I have heard of You by the hearing of the ear, But now my eye sees You. Therefore I abhor myself, And repent in dust and ashes" (Job 42:3–6). Though Job had been a man of integrity, God's integrity far exceeded that of himself. God alone is holy, and even our greatest accomplishments on this earth are but waste in the presence of His holiness.

Chapter 6

Focus: A strength is not the same thing as a calling. And being good at something you dislike doesn't mean that you have to do it all the time.

1. "I said in my heart, 'God shall judge the righteous and the wicked, For there is a time there for every purpose and for every work'" (Ecclesiastes 3:17). The writer of Ecclesiastes goes on to say that there is a time for every season under heaven. Your job or position may be a perfect fit for you at this time in life, but five years down the road God may be calling you to something new. It's important that we stay obedient to the voice of the Lord in our lives.

2. "I, therefore, the prisoner of the Lord, beseech you to walk worthy of the calling with which you were called, with all lowliness and gentleness, with longsuffering, bearing with one another in love, endeavoring to keep the unity of the Spirit in the bond of peace. There is one body and one Spirit, just as you were called in one hope of your calling; one Lord, one faith, one baptism; one God and Father of all, who is above all, and through all, and in you all" (Ephesians 4:1–6). We are all called to bring glory to God.

3. God has given each of us passions and desires, and each of us has things we do that make us feel as if we're significant. When we connect those dots in our lives we can find the sweet spots, where our gifts and desires unite and we both glorify God and enjoy Him.

4. "May He grant you according to your heart's desire, And fulfill all your purpose. We will rejoice in your salvation, And in the name of our God we will set up our banners! May the Lord fulfill all your petitions" (Psalm 20:4–5). God gives us our desires, and He listens when we ask Him for help in fulfilling them. Don't dismiss those longings in your spirit as the idealistic dreams of youth, but consider them as valid options for a life that glorifies God.

5. "But as God has distributed to each one, as the Lord has called each one, so let him walk. And so I ordain in all the churches. Was anyone called while circumcised? Let him not become uncircumcised. Was anyone called while uncircumcised? Let him not be circumcised. Circumcision is nothing and uncircumcision is nothing, but keeping the commandments of God is what matters. Let each one remain in the same calling in which he was called. Were you called while a slave? Do not be concerned about it; but if you can be made free, rather use it. For he who is called in the Lord while a slave is the Lord's freedman. Likewise he who is called while free is Christ's slave. You were bought at a price; do not become slaves of men. Brethren, let each one remain with God in that state in which he was called" (1 Corinthians 7:17–24). We don't have to fear God's calling in our lives. It doesn't mean that we must abandon all that we know and love. We can each find a way to use our strengths and gifts right where we are. And, at the same time, if we feel frustrated or misplaced in life we have the freedom to explore the opportunities God gives us in all the world to find our niche.

6. God has given all of us unique gifts and strengths. And, there are a wide variety of tasks that need to be done each day for society to keep on functioning at a good pace. We need teachers, trash collectors, doctors, factory workers, fashion designers, parole officers, and hospice workers. Some of these jobs may sound wonderful to us and others horrible, but each is necessary.

7. It's possible to find our fulfillment in other places — at home, in community, or in religious fellowship — rather than "on the job."

8. You may be great at telling someone really difficult truths in love or comforting someone who has lost a loved one. Those are not fun things to do, but we all need someone who is good at them.

Chapter 7

Focus: Weakness is not something we should be ashamed of or try to hide. Instead we should imagine ourselves as God describes us so often—as lambs in the shepherd's arms.

1. "No, much rather, those members of the body which seem to be weaker are necessary" (1 Corinthians 12:22). Paul tells us we need both weak and strong members.

2. "Watch and pray, lest you enter into temptation. The spirit indeed is willing, but the flesh is weak" (Matthew 26:41 and Mark 14:38). "For I determined not to know anything among you except Jesus Christ and Him crucified. I was with you in weakness, in fear, and in much trembling. And my speech and my preaching were not with persuasive words of human wisdom, but in demonstration of the Spirit and of power, that your faith should not be in the wisdom of men but in the power of God" (1 Corinthians 2:2–5). "For we do not have a High Priest who cannot sympathize with our weaknesses, but was in all points tempted as we are, yet without sin" (Hebrews 4:15).

3. "Likewise the Spirit also helps in our weaknesses. For we do not know what we should pray for as we ought, but the Spirit Himself makes intercession for us with groanings which cannot be uttered" (Romans 8:26).

4. "I have shown you in every way, by laboring like this, that you must support the weak. And remember the words of the Lord Jesus, that He said, 'It is more blessed to give than to receive'" (Acts 20:35). "Receive one who is weak in the faith, but not to disputes over doubtful things" (Romans 14:1). "We then who are strong ought to bear with the scruples of the weak, and not to please ourselves" (Romans 15:1). "Now we exhort you, brethren, warn those who are unruly, comfort the fainthearted, uphold the weak, be patient with all" (1 Thessalonians 5:14).

5. "Now concerning things offered to idols: We know that we all have knowledge. Knowledge puffs up, but love edifies. And if anyone thinks that he knows anything, he knows nothing yet as he ought to know. But if anyone loves God, this one is known by Him.

Therefore concerning the eating of things offered to idols, we know that an idol is nothing in the world, and that there is no other God but one. For even if there are so-called gods, whether in heaven or on earth (as there are many gods and many lords), yet for us there is one God, the Father, of whom are all things, and we for Him; and one Lord Jesus Christ, through whom are all things, and through whom we live.

However, there is not in everyone that knowledge; for some, with consciousness of the idol, until now eat it as a thing offered to an idol; and their conscience, being weak, is defiled. But food does not commend us to God; for neither if we eat are we the better, nor if we do not eat are we the worse.

But beware lest somehow this liberty of yours become a stumbling block to those who are weak. For if anyone sees you who have knowledge eating in an idol's temple, will not the conscience of him who is weak be emboldened to eat those things offered to idols? And because of your knowledge shall the weak brother perish, for whom Christ died? But when you thus sin against the brethren, and wound their weak conscience, you sin against Christ. Therefore, if food makes my brother stumble, I will never again eat meat, lest I make my brother stumble" (1 Corinthians 8).

Paul begins by warning them against prideful knowledge. When a person is coming from a know-it-all attitude, it's very difficult to get through to her and also it's highly unlikely that she would adopt an attitude of compassion toward her weaker sisters.

6. "But beware lest somehow this liberty of yours become a stumbling block to those who are weak" (1 Corinthians 8:9).

7. It's important to remember that the debate is not bad, in itself. But arrogance and disregard for the spiritual health of those you're in community with is bad. So if you find yourself in a debate over spiritual issues, keep your focus on the spiritual health of your community more than getting caught in "right fighting," where your only goal is to win the argument.

8. Answers

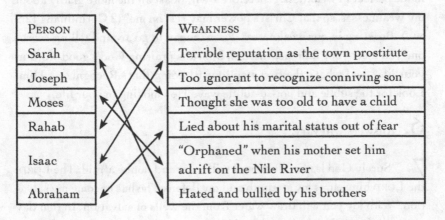

PERSON		WEAKNESS
Sarah		Terrible reputation as the town prostitute
Joseph		Too ignorant to recognize conniving son
Moses		Thought she was too old to have a child
Rahab		Lied about his marital status out of fear
Isaac		"Orphaned" when his mother set him adrift on the Nile River
Abraham		Hated and bullied by his brothers

9. "These all died in faith" (Hebrews 11:13).

Chapter 8

Focus: If you find that you are relying on your own strengths, and not God's, to accomplish all the things you have on your to-do list, it might be time to reconsider your priorities.

1. Answers will vary.

2. "The Sovereign Lord is my strength; he makes my feet like the feet of a deer, he enables me to tread on the heights" (Habakkuk 3:19 NIV). When we're at the depths of overwhelming emotions, we feel frustrated, tired, and helpless. But God has already given us what we need to soar to the heights and succeed in our efforts.

3. "It is God who arms me with strength and keeps my way secure" (2 Samuel 22:33 NIV).

4. "My flesh and my heart may fail, but *God is the strength of my heart and my portion forever*" (Psalm 73:26 NIV, emphasis mine).

5. "But he said to me, 'My grace is sufficient for you, for my power is made perfect in weakness.' Therefore I will boast all the more gladly about my weaknesses, so that Christ's power may rest on me" (2 Corinthians 12:9 NIV). Boasting in our weaknesses doesn't mean to go around telling everyone you meet your failings. Instead, it means praising God's good work in your life. And what's the first step toward doing that? Recognizing Him. Look for the subtle and not-so-subtle ways He's moving in your life.

6. Answers will vary.

7. "'Surely God is my salvation; I will trust and not be afraid. The LORD, the LORD himself, is my strength and my defense; he has become my salvation.' With joy you will draw water from the wells of salvation. In that day you will say: 'Give praise to the Lord, proclaim his name; make known

among the nations what he has done, and proclaim that his name is exalted. Sing to the Lord, for he has done glorious things; let this be known to all the world'" (Isaiah 12:2–5 NIV).

Chapter 9

Focus: We should always be seeking new ways to honor and glorify God with our lives, and if we find new talents we may find more opportunities to encourage and inspire even more people to worship Christ.

1. Answers will vary.

2. Think outside the box as you answer this question. If you learn to paint you might be able to create murals for your church's nursery, but you also may meet some people in your classes who you can introduce to Christ.

3. "Be diligent to present yourself approved to God, a worker who does not need to be ashamed, rightly dividing the word of truth" (2 Timothy 2:15). By studying the Scriptures we will not be ashamed.

4. "And let us not grow weary while doing good, for in due season we shall reap if we do not lose heart" (Galatians 6:9).

5. Proverbs criticizes the lazy person and praises the one who is diligent to work hard, practicing her strengths in her life. "The hand of the diligent will rule, But the lazy man will be put to forced labor" (12:24). "The lazy man does not roast what he took in hunting, But diligence is man's precious possession" (12:27). "The soul of a lazy man desires, and has nothing; But the soul of the diligent shall be made rich" (13:4). "A lazy man buries his hand in the bowl, And will not so much as bring it to his mouth again" (19:24). "The lazy man will not plow because of winter; He will beg during harvest and have nothing" (20:4). "The desire of the lazy man kills him, For his hands refuse to labor" (21:25).

6. "That we should no longer be children, tossed to and fro and carried about with every wind of doctrine, by the trickery of men, in the cunning

craftiness of deceitful plotting, but, speaking the truth in love, may grow up in all things into Him who is the head — Christ — from whom the whole body, joined and knit together by what every joint supplies, according to the effective working by which every part does its share, causes growth of the body for the edifying of itself in love" (Ephesians 4:14–16). When every one does her part, the community is edified and unified in Christ.

7. Answers will vary.

Chapter 10

Focus: Before we can embrace the strength and courage God offers us, we must get rid of our old perceptions and see what Scripture has to tell us about who we are in God's eyes.

1. Answers will vary.

2. The Spirit you received does not make you slaves, so that you live in fear again; rather, the Spirit you received brought about your adoption to sonship. And by him we cry, 'Abba, Father.' The spirit himself testifies with our spirit that we are God's children. Now if we are children, then we are heirs—heirs of God and co-heirs with Christ." (Romans 8:15–17 NIV). This passage tells us that God considers us His children — that He has adopted us into His family and we are heirs to all that He is and all that He has.

3. As beloved children of God, we have already been given the ability to have all these attributes — love, joy, peace, patience, kindness, goodness, faithfulness, gentleness, and self-control. These are not unattainable attributes, but are there for us to embrace. Through Christ, we have already been given them — we just need to claim them. These are not attributes that we need to get in our own strength — that would be impossible. Instead, we need only to ask God to help us claim them and use them.

4. "The Lord gives strength to his people" (Psalm 29:11 NIV). Point out that it is the Lord who gives us strength — He doesn't demand that we be strong for Him; He doesn't expect us to be able to do it on our own. He is the Giver and Sustainer.

5. Answers

Scripture	Person	Action
1 Samuel 25	Abigail	Through quick thinking and bold and confident action, Abigail diffused David's anger and saved her family.
1 Samuel 17:45–50	David	David miraculously defeated a powerful enemy in the name of the Lord.
Joshua 2	Rahab	Rahab risked her life to hide the Israelite spies, saving her family from destruction.
Esther 5:1–8, 7:1–5	Esther	Esther risked her position as queen to ask the king to save her people, the Jews, from sure annihilation.

6. "Then the disciples came to Jesus in private and asked, 'Why couldn't we drive [the demon] out?' He replied, 'Because you have so little faith. Truly I tell you, if you have faith as small as a mustard seed, you can say to this mountain, "Move from here to there" and it will move. Nothing will be impossible for you.'" (Matthew 17:19–20 NIV).

7. Answers here will vary, but often we tend to think that our gifts are not as important or as useful as someone else's gifts. If you find that your members struggle with realizing the importance of their gifts, encourage them with the following verses. "We have different gifts, according to the grace given to each of us." (Romans 12:6 NIV). "Each of you should use whatever gift you have received to serve others, as faithful stewards of God's grace in its various forms" (1 Peter 4:10 NIV).

8. Answers will vary.

Chapter 11

Focus: When we use our gifts and talents in service of him, sacrificially giving of our time and resources to further God's influence on another's life, we are celebrating our strengths.

1. Answers will vary.

2. When a woman celebrates her strengths she is fulfilling the first question and answer of the Westminster Catechism, which says the purpose of man's life is to glorify God and enjoy Him forever. When we embrace the gifts He's given us and use them to spread His truth in the world, and enjoy ourselves in the process, people will be attracted to God's spirit in us.

3. When we take the time to enjoy God we are filled with Him. He invades every part of our lives and we become more like Him.

4. c, e, b, a, f, d

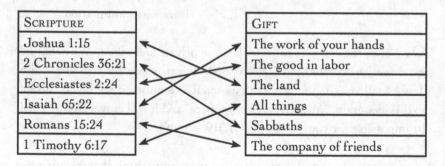

SCRIPTURE		GIFT
Joshua 1:15		The work of your hands
2 Chronicles 36:21		The good in labor
Ecclesiastes 2:24		The land
Isaiah 65:22		All things
Romans 15:24		Sabbaths
1 Timothy 6:17		The company of friends

5. "'Go therefore and make disciples of all the nations, baptizing them in the name of the Father and of the Son and of the Holy Spirit, teaching them to observe all things that I have commanded you; and lo, I am with you always, even to the end of the age.' Amen" (Matthew 28:19–20). Answers will vary.

6. Answers will vary.

7. Answers will vary.

Chapter 12

Focus: Listen for His voice to guide you in the way you should go.

1. Answers will vary.

2. "You shall walk after the Lord your God and fear Him, and keep His commandments and obey His voice; you shall serve Him and hold fast to Him" (Deuteronomy 13:4). "God thunders marvelously with His voice; He does great things which we cannot comprehend" (Job 37:5). "Oh come, let us worship and bow down; Let us kneel before the Lord our Maker. For He is our God, And we are the people of His pasture, And the sheep of His hand. Today, if you will hear His voice: 'Do not harden your hearts, as in the rebellion, As in the day of trial in the wilderness'" (Psalm 95:6–8). "And the sound of the wings of the cherubim was heard even in the outer court, like the voice of Almighty God when He speaks" (Ezekiel 10:5). "Most assuredly, I say to you, the hour is coming, and now is, when the dead will hear the voice of the Son of God; and those who hear will live" (John 5:25).

3. Answers will vary. Samples follow:

Person	Calling	Strength
Abraham	Leave home	Adventuresome spirit
Esther	Save the Jews	Beauty and smarts
Solomon	Build the temple	Wealth, Strategy
John the Baptist	Prepare the way for Jesus	Selflessness
Jonah	Take the gospel to Ninevah	Perseverance

4. Answers will vary.

5. Answers will vary.

6. Answers will vary.

7. Answers will vary.